HOW TO BE AN AIRSOFT SNIPER

A COMPLETE STEP - BY-STEP GUIDE TO BECOMING A SNIPER

HOW TO BE AN AIRSOFT SNIPER

A complete step-by-step guide
To becoming a sniper

By Mark Laxton

Table of Contents

The Skills of a Sniper

Shooting
Fire Position Checklist
Things to Avoid
Safety Regulations
Shooting Conditions
Wind
Temperature
Mirage
Humidity
Rain
Light
Clothing

Fire Positions
Standing
Kneeling
Sitting
Laying Back
The Hawkins Position

Camouflage & Concealment
Use of cover
Dead Ground
Movement
Noise
Isolated cover
Soft cover
Background
Silhouette
Shadows
Foliage

Movement
The Monkey run
The Leopard crawl
The Stomach crawl

Observation
Target Identification

Judging Distance
Unit of measure
Appearance method
Halving method
Bracketing method
Squad average
Binocular/Scope Graticules

Introduction

Welcome to 'How to be an Airsoft Sniper'.

This book has been designed to help you develop and improve the necessary skills and tactics it takes to become an affective and highly efficient Airsoft sniper.

As the author of this book I have combined, not only my experience of being an airsoft player but also my knowledge and expertise of being an ex-Military Sniper Marksman. I spent several years in the British Armed Forces. During which time I served operationally in many different countries and various hostile environments. During my service I served as a sniper marksman within the reconnaissance platoon.

To master such a high level of field craft skills and weapons training within the military, I had to undergo several weeks of very intense and rigorous training, all of which I will now share with you.

The step by step instructions and advice that I will provide you with, will guide you through the training of a real life sniper and yet remain relevant to the equipment that you will use as well as the rules and regulations of an Airsoft game.

You will learn all of the tricks of the trade, some of which may not be found elsewhere, all with the aim to help you become one of the most valuable assets of an Airsoft team, The Sniper.

Whilst you may already think that you are quite an effective player, there are many ways in which you can improve your skills to ensure that you remain undetected whilst taking out other players with a single shot, all of which are contained within this book.

The book itself is laid out to provide an easy to follow step by step guide, as to what you will need to know, as well as the equipment you will require and how to use it effectively.

Read each section carefully and take relevant notes on important key subjects as well as any TOP TIPS this may help you remember them in future.

The best way to be successful in what you are wishing to achieve, is to take time to prepare fully and ensure you have not only learned the basic information necessary but also learned from people that have inside information as well as tips and advice they have gained through experience as this may not be openly available anywhere else.

What is Airsoft?

Airsoft was invented in Japan in the 1970's and is a leisure activity in which people use replica firearms that fire round plastic pellets, in an attempt to hit their opponents and eliminate them from the game. The game relies on every players honesty and whenever hit anywhere on the body, they should declare themselves hit to an umpire or whoever's in charge and return to their base.

Airsoft games may consist of any number of players and teams in various environments and over any specified period of time.
Games could be anything from a few individual players playing indoors for only a few hours, to a huge outdoor battlefield played by a number of different teams over a number of days and nights.
Some games may be designed around the re-enactment of historical battles and military operations or maybe even close quarter confrontations in built up urban areas such as the likes of Police armed response teams may deal with.

In most cases, it's very likely that not only the replica weapons will be designed to be as close to the real thing as possible but also a range of clothing, equipment and tactics will be utilised in order to create the most realistic experience possible.

Due to the nature of such an activity, there are obviously strict laid down legal restrictions on possessing such weapons and rules and regulations specific to game play. These are for everyone's benefit and the safety of every person involved in the event.

The details of such safety restrictions regarding maximum muzzle velocity of weapons and minimum distance for engaging other players will be covered within the relevant sections of this book as well as the necessary safety equipment required to play an Airsoft game.

Please stick to these guidelines at all times to ensure not only the safety of others but also yourself and you will enjoy the excellent experience and enjoyment that Airsoft provides.

What is a Sniper?

A sniper is an expert marksman and observer, with the skills and ability to locate an enemy or target where ever they are and however well concealed. They may need to lie in wait for the perfect opportunity to take the shot or they may choose to stalk up on the enemy whilst remaining undetected. Then eliminate the target with a single shot!

A sniper is able to gather valuable information on enemy movements and equipment through the use of their expert skills in observing, interpreting and accurately recording information.

They can observe without being observed - kill without being killed.

Ideally as a sniper, you should train and operate in pairs. One of you will be responsible for taking the shot, whilst the other will assist in observing the target, judging distance and wind speed as well as keeping a watchful eye on your surrounding area for signs of enemy movement and protecting the shooter if necessary.

You may be deployed on your own to achieve a specific task or objective or you may form part of a team or section.
If there are a number of snipers being used, you would ideally be sited with interlocking fields of view and arcs of fire, so that all possible areas of enemy movement are always covered and communications between each sniper is maintained at all times.

Due to the limitations of Airsoft equipment it may seem obvious that there are certain areas such as the difference in the weapons capabilities including distances and sight adjustments for wind speed etc. However the vast majority of skills, equipment and tactics that a military sniper would use, are very useful and in some cases, absolutely essential for you to become an excellent Airsoft sniper.

How are Snipers used?

A sniper is an invaluable asset to any Airsoft team and used correctly,
They could mean the difference between a team's success or failure.
There are a number of different roles for which a sniper may be utilised to great
effect, these are;

You may be deployed for reconnaissance purposes, to observe targets, enemy
movement and gather valuable information that can then be fed back to your team.

You may be given a specific target that you are required to eliminate such as the
person in charge of the other team or any other target that may play an important
role or provide the other team with a distinct advantage.

You could be used in conjunction with your team or in a section/fire group of your
team with the aim to take out specific targets just prior to an assault or ambush.

You could be working in liaison with other sniper teams, with interlocking fields of
view and designated boundaries, to cover a route in which the other team are
known to or are likely to use.

Your skills and expertise could be put to the test against an enemy sniper in a
counter-sniper operation.

If in a defensive role you could be deployed to provide an observation post covering your own team's defences with the aim to prevent the opposing team successfully capturing your flag for example.

As a sniper you can actually halt the advance of a whole battle group or large team by systematically taking out targets such as the Oic (Officer in charge) Radio signalman, any heavy arms fire etc or slow the assault of the opposing team with harassing fire whilst your own team withdraws.

Could you be a Sniper?

So, let's find out if you think that you have what it takes to be a good Airsoft sniper?

Obviously, your physical condition and some other effecting factors will not play as much importance to your performance, as they would in a real life combat situation but the closer you are to these guidelines, the more you will improve your effectiveness and chances of success.

Height and Weight

You may be surprised to find that snipers come in all shapes and sizes, I personally stand at 6'10" (although I think I may have started shrinking a bit now I'm getting older, maybe I'll be normal height by the time I'm 80?)
People would sometimes ask how I could be a sniper, being my size.
Well it goes without saying really, it made no difference as the majority of the time is spent on your belt buckle as you are crawling or lying in wait for that one perfect opportunity to take the shot.

Physical Condition

Whatever size or shape you are, it is essential that you maintain a high level of fitness, maybe more so than other team members. You may need to travel long distances carrying kit and be deployed for long periods of time without a rest. You may be left behind by your team to provide harassing fire as they withdraw, after which you will need to get out of there pretty quick as the other team will be closer and hot on your trail.

Smoking

As with most physical activities, it's advised that you don't smoke purely for health reasons, I actually know plenty of guys I served with in the armed forces, that were among some of the fittest people I've ever known and yet they smoked like a chimney, however as a sniper it's not only a health and fitness issue but it can also have a detrimental effect on your performance.

If you smoke whilst playing a game or carrying out an objective you may have been given, you can may make others aware of your presence due to the smell of smoke being carried downwind, at night time the glow of a cigarette being inhaled is surprisingly bright and can be seen through woodland at quite some distance, discarded cigarette butts will give away your chosen firing/observation position, making it easier for your opponents or enemy snipers to locate you in future games.

As well as all this, if you are playing for long periods of time and restraining from smoking, you may find yourself becoming fidgety and anxious which will then affect your performance and shooting ability.

Eyesight

It may be quite obvious that you must have excellent eyesight for shooting and observing enemy movements at great distances but this is not the only reason.

If you are required to wear glasses or contact lenses you could be a liability to yourself.
Wearing glasses could give away your position by reflecting the sunlight off the lenses and the loss or damage to glasses or contact lenses could render you inoperable or unable to perform at your maximum capability.

Personal attributes

In some ways snipers are very different to an average soldier or in this case other team members. They are often found to be quite confidently quiet and very comfortable with working alone. Some people also have a natural way or feel for adapting to and easily navigating through different environments.
Whilst other team members will be running around and all laying down fire at the same time or taking pot shots at opponents as a fire group or section. This may result in them being unsure of a confirmed hit due to the amount of other weapons being fired.
 As a sniper on the other hand, you will be taking your time to move silently and locating targets whilst remaining unseen, then calmly and deliberately taking a single well aimed shot to eliminate your chosen target. You will not be left unsure of a confirmed hit as it's likely you will see you pellet hit the target through your sights then you will stealthily move from your position leaving no trace that you were ever there.

You are required to possess a great deal of patience as you may be lying in wait for long periods of time, as other team players are running around and most likely getting more kills than you will during the game but there is no better feeling than when you locate your target and successfully eliminate him then disappear leaving the enemy in a panic and wondering what the hell just happened.

You also need to be confident and able to make the correct decision within a split second if things don't go quite according to plan. This could mean the difference between you continuing the game or being eliminated.

You also need to have an above average intelligence and common sense. I find it's quite rare for people to have both, they usually have one or the other. The amount of times I've met people that hold very important jobs or positions that require an extremely high level of education and intelligence but when it comes to some very simple tasks, they don't have a clue? Well it just so happens, you need both!

You need to retain information and useful details on things such as, the battlefield ground and terrain; opponent's numbers and equipment etc. This information may be used for your team to plan attacks.

An expert knowledge both theoretical and practical of equipment, field craft and tactics is a great advantage in influencing your decisions whilst carrying out your objectives.
If you know what the other team is likely to do or how they are likely to plan their movements or make use of equipment, you are always one step ahead of them.

Shooting Ability

As you may expect, one of the key skills of a sniper is your accuracy of shooting. There's no point in having all of these skills and finding the perfect firing position, waiting for hours only to take the shot and end up shooting the wrong target by accident. Remember: whilst every good shot may not be a sniper, every sniper must be a good shot.

You must be totally familiar with your chosen sniper rifle and its sights, to the point where it feels like an extension of your own body. You must ensure that you keep the weapon in pristine condition and clean all working parts, the last thing you need is a stoppage or miss-fire.
Your sights must be correctly zeroed and you will learn about adjustments for different conditions and wind speed in later sections of this book.

Sniper Equipment

Depending on which type of Airsoft game you take part in and the environment the game is played in may influence you in which role you wish to choose.
These roles may vary from being a member of an Assault team or as part of your team's defences. Or, as you are reading this book it's likely that you are thinking about operating as a sniper or wishing to learn how to improve your sniper skills.

As well as all of the skills and tactics that you will need to develop, you will also need to ensure that you have all of the necessary equipment and know how to use it all to the best of your ability.
Not only will you need the correct equipment to carry out your role proficiently but you will also need to make sure that you are wearing the correct personal protective equipment whilst playing Airsoft so as to prevent yourself against any injuries.

The following kit list will provide you with all of the items of equipment that you will need.
(Note: not all of these items are essential but the more you have the better you will be prepared) I will explain how to use each piece of kit and detail their statistics and capabilities which I also advise you to try and remember.

Airsoft Sniper Equipment

- Ghillie Suit / Camouflage Clothing
- Hood/Face Veil
- Eye/Face Protection
- Gloves
- Boots
- Binoculars
- Sniper Spotting Scope
- Rifle + Sling + Ammunition
- Telescopic Sight
- Night Vision
- Silencer
- Side Arm + Ammunition
- Radio Comms/Headset or Earpiece
- Camouflage Cream
- Watch
- Compass
- Protractor
- Water Proof Pen + Notebook
- Drinking Water

The Ghillie Suit

As a sniper you will need to purchase or better still, make your own ghillie suit. It's very simple to make but can be quite time consuming, although the more time and effort you put into making one, the longer it will last you and the more it will aid you in staying concealed and undetected.

The purpose of wearing a ghillie suit is to help provide you with the means of camouflaging yourself and blending into your environment. This will assist you in staying hidden from your opponents and enemy snipers.

Design

The suit is designed to break up the distinct outline and contours of the human body, which is quite easily done by attaching various manmade materials.
The use and placement of various coloured materials is also essential to distort the image and prevent it being identifiable. If the colours used were all too similar then they would blend together to create the appearance of a solid object.
Colours used should mainly be light and dark browns, some natural greens and maybe even some black.

When designing the suit it maybe an idea to draw a suit first and play around with the colour schemes and placements and try to keep them fairly random. Anything to organised or symmetrical will not look natural. If you squint whilst looking at the design or finished product it shouldn't be very easy to identify the outline or solid mass of the object. In the dark you shouldn't be able to make out the shape of a human silhouette.

You should also include a way of attaching materials from your natural surroundings such as grass, leaves, shrubs and other vegetation to your suit. This can easily be done by connecting strips of black elastic to your suit, sewn at either end and leaving a gap for you to stuff your natural camouflage into.
This would be done regularly as you move from one area to another.
As your natural surroundings change, so should your camouflage to match it.

How to Make a Ghillie Suit

Materials Required:

Camouflage Clothing (Ideally Rural Colours/Disruptive Pattern Material consisting of a Jacket, Preferably Hooded. Trousers, Hat or Balaclava, Boots and Gloves).
Hessian Sacks/Sandbags/Jute or Burlap (Preferably old/used and dirty)
Scrim Netting
Vehicle Camouflage Netting
Any Old Army Green T-Shirts
Strips Of Elastic

Wire Brush
Glue Gun/Strong Glue
Needle and Thread
Sharp Knife/Strong Scissors

TOP TIP: Also as an optional extra, I would advise you to add some form of padding that you could sew into the inside elbow and knee areas of your Ghillie suit, to provide you with added comfort, as you will be spending a lot of time crawling or in a stationary fire position.

Step 1

Find a good area to work and ensure it's well ventilated as you will be using strong solvents. Then take your clothing and lay it out from top to bottom and set up the materials you have to use.

Step 2

Ok. You're all set. Firstly start by taking the sand bags/ hessian sacks and cut them down one side and along the bottom so that you can open it all out into one flat piece of material. (These should preferably be old/used and dirty and slightly different shades of browns or greens)
Then take some scissors and cut strips from the bottom to a few inches from the top, each strip should be around 1-2 inches wide. Once this is done take the wire brush and comb down each strip applying pressure, this will gradually start too fray and separate the strands of the material. It ends up with a solid strip along the top which will later be attached to the clothing and leave the strips of material loosely hanging.

Note: The more sand bags and sacks you prepare in this way the better your suit will be, this is probably the hardest and most time consuming part of creating the ghillie suit.

Step 3

Next, take a selection of any old T-shirts or other material coloured dark green or brown and also cut into frayed strips leaving a strip along the top which will be glued to the suit.
Along with all this material do the same with scrim netting and any vehicle camo netting you can get your hands on.

Step 4

Now, using a glue gun and a strong glue, attach some of the pieces of material to your Hat/Balaclava + the hood of your jacket if it has one, pay particular attention to the top, sides and rear so as to break up the outline of your head and ensure that your view will not be obstructed.

TOP TIP: I personally found that an adapted balaclava was perfect for this, it leaves you with the option of pulling the top down off your head, similar to a hood whilst the chin and neck area keep it in place.
It's then very easy to pull back over your head when needed and fits well around your face.
If you choose to you may also attach a face veil made up of such material as scrim netting, this would still allow you to see through it but would cover your face or the top of the sight when in a fire position.

Step 5

Next, we'll move on to the Jacket. Lay your jacket face down and use the glue gun and strong glue to attach the various coloured materials to the back of your jacket, paying particular attention to the shoulder areas to help break up that distinct outline of the head and shoulders area.
Also cover the outer arms and leave the material hanging down, so that it then fills the space between the body and outstretched arms.
It's advised that you also cover areas on the front of the jacket, although it's not as necessary to do as much as on the back. This is because when you are stalking the enemy or in a stationary fire position it's very likely that you will be on your belly.
Too much on the front may also impede your movement and snag on things as you are crawling.
As well as adding these materials, also stitch a number of black elastic strips all over the jacket in various sizes, these will be used to attach elements of natural camouflage to your suit as you progress through different types of cover.

As I mentioned briefly before, I'd advice sewing some form of padding to the inside of the elbows to provide added extra comfort.

Step 6

Moving onto your trousers/pants, you should do the same as you did for your jacket with both the materials and elastic strips. Make sure that some material hangs down over your boots but not too much, so as to prevent the possibility of standing on it or tripping.

As I mentioned briefly before, I'd advice sewing some form of padding to the inside of the Knees to provide added extra comfort.

Step 7

Remember to camouflage your boots with small pieces of material, it's surprising how much a pair of un-camouflaged boots can stand out, the solid black colour doesn't blend in well with most rural natural environments.

As well as your boots, also camouflage your gloves and it's advisable that you cut the tips off the finger and thumb of your glove so as to make it easier to fire.

Step 8

This should now be your ghillie suit complete.
However to add the finishing touch you may want to find a nice big muddy puddle and splatter your ghillie suit in mud and drag it along the ground then leave it to dry.
If you wanted to go one step further, which is what some people do when stalking game/animals to disguise their scent, you can roll your suit around in manure.

Although if you do this for playing airsoft, you may find that no one chooses you to be on their team!

If you're working in a sniper team you may find other uses for your spotter, such as helping you support your rifle which will aid the stability of your aim

Eye/Face Protection

One of the most, if not THE most important pieces of equipment that you will need to play airsoft safely is the correct form of protection to guard your eyes, teeth and face against injury from airsoft pellets.

Warning: Ensure that you always wear the correct protective equipment whilst playing airsoft and avoid removing it whilst in play.
Taking off your goggles or facemask during play, even for only a few minutes to wipe away sweat could result in you being shot in the face unprotected.
Being shot with an airsoft pellet could seriously damage your eyesight and possibly lead to blindness and a bb pellet hitting you in the teeth could easily break a tooth.

That said, there are generally 3 types of protection that you can choose from;

Facemask

A full face mask is obviously the best form of protection and they come in all different cool designs. Although this is the safest option you may find that it causes you to sweat more and some people may find it a little claustrophobic. If the mask is too close to the face it could cause a build up carbon dioxide (which is what you exhale) and impede your breathing slightly.
However if you find one that fits well I'd recommend getting it so as to avoid any injuries.

Goggles

Goggles provide an excellent level of protection for the eyes and are less restrictive than a full face mask although the rest of your face and teeth are at risk of injury.

Protective Glasses

Whilst glasses protect your eyes from most angles, they do leave your eyes
Unprotected from the gaps at the sides, as well as the rest of your face and teeth.

Note: With any of the above mentioned forms of eye protection, unless the lenses
are mesh then it is very likely that they will steam up. This can be prevented by
applying an anti-fog agent to them prior to wearing them.

Gloves and Boots

Although you may think that your hands and feet are so small that they are unlikely to be seen, you'd be surprised how much a solid black pair of gloves or boots can give away your position.

Gloves

The gloves are easily camouflaged and provide added protection against pellets. Some gloves are already available in a camouflage pattern and a single strip of elastic on the back of the hand or wrist can be added to attach natural foliage. I'd also recommend fingerless gloves or at least the tips of the forefinger and thumb of the firing hand to be removed. This allows more ease of operating the safety switch etc as well as increasing the feel of movement of the trigger.

Boots

A decent pair of boots is vital. The boots should not only provide good ankle support but they need to be comfortable as well as lightweight and waterproof (A Gore-Tex liner is advised) They should keep your feet dry but also allow your feet to breath.
The material should be resistant to abrasions, scuffs and tears whilst crawling and dry quickly if they become wet.
The soles should provide a good grip and allow downhill breaking as well as side hill traction to aid in climbing steep slopes.

Binoculars

As a sniper, it's important that you are an expert observer and able to use the equipment available to you, to the best of its ability. There are 2 such aids to observing that you should use and know how and when each of these will aid you the most.

Whether you are trying to locate your opponent's position or stalking them, observing your opponents and their movements or defending your own base. A good pair of binoculars will aid you greatly in doing this.

They are light and convenient to carry and provide you with a wide field of view so that you can scan a large area quite quickly.

Not only will they assist you in locating your opponents but some binoculars come equipped with range finders, these will give you massive advantage in judging the distance to your target prior to taking a shot and making the necessary adjustments. You will find that different binoculars offer different levels of magnification; ideally you need the minimum of x6 magnification. However, at longer distances and to see objects in greater detail you will require a spotter scope which I will cover next. At night time binoculars will perform better than sniper scopes but if money is no object, then nothing beats night vision equipment which I will also discuss.

You should make sure that you are completely familiar with the focusing of the binoculars, and ensure that you make a habit of holding them with the forefinger and thumb of each hand, forming an OK shape around the end of the binoculars and the other fingers providing a shelter over the lenses. This will prevent any light being reflected off the lenses and giving away your position.

TOP TIP: They should always have the lenses covered when not in use and are usually carried via a sling around the neck although you may find they are left swinging like this, so you may want to tuck them into your jacket.

Spotter Scope

A sniper spotter scope is excellent for searching the ground at greater distances usually providing at least x20 magnification and can pick out objects that are lightly camouflaged or in shadows far better than binoculars. Although due to the smaller field of view they are not as easy to use.
As with binoculars, the lenses can easily reflect light and give away your position from a great distance. Therefore carry them in a case or with the lens covered and make sure the ray shade is fully extended or make a ray shade if you scope doesn't have one.
Unlike binoculars spotter scopes sometimes need additional support due to being longer, this provides added steadiness and accuracy and can easily be done using a stand or resting the end of the scope on some cover or lying back and using your knee for support.

Airsoft Sniper Rifle & Ammunition

Obviously one of the most important pieces of equipment that a sniper needs is a very reliable long range rifle with a telescopic sight, sling and ammunition.
There's a very wide range of sniper rifle makes and models and an Airsoft replica, for just about every one of them.

When it comes to their performance, you will need to consider a number of factors such as the legal requirements of muzzle velocity (How powerful the gun is and how many feet per second the pellet/BB can travel) as well as the construction, operating system and ammunition.

Construction and Legal Requirements

Airsoft sniper rifles should have a long metal barrel and the smaller the diameter of the inner bore, the better. This will ensure that you have a more consistent long range shot by providing you with the best muzzle velocity, which influences how many feet per second your pellet/BB will travel.
Generally this would be 300-350 fps indoors and 350-450fps outdoors.
As with all airsoft guns the barrel should have an orange tip, this is for legal reasons and should never be removed. As airsoft guns are such good replicas of the real thing, this is sometimes the only thing that identifies them as replicas. Removing it could potentially cause you all kinds of trouble with the law.
For enhanced realism and slightly more accuracy you might choose to opt for a bolt-action rifle which tends to be quieter as they have less working parts.

Hop-Up

You should also ensure that your rifle has an adjustable Hop-Up
(High Operation Power Up) device.
This is often a piece of rubber inside the rear of the barrel that causes the pellet to backspin as it passes it. It should be adjustable to suit the needs of the player's preference.
The purpose of the Hop-Up is to create the pellet to backspin so that it travels further and doesn't gradually drop over greater distances and it should also help minimise the effects of wind on the pellet.

Operating Systems

Spring Action
The most basic form of airsoft operation is the spring action which means that the rifle is required to be manually cocked after each shot to re-load another pellet.

Gas Operated
Gas operated system guns allow semi-automatic or fully-automatic fire, which means that you don't have to keep cocking the weapon after each shot. However there are 2 types of gas operated airsoft guns.
The non-blowback system requires the gas cartridge to be reloaded after firing several round magazines and it has a fixed cocking lever.
(You will therefore need to carry spare gas cartridges)
For a more realistic firing experience the gas blowback system allows the cocking lever to move back and forth after each shot, like a real rifle and this causes you to feel the recoil when firing.

Electric (AEG - Automatic Electric Gun)
For the ultimate operating system an electric airsoft gun can fire upto 3000 rounds without having to be recharged and they are extremely reliable.
The gun is powered by a battery and can fire 750 rounds per minute on fully automatic and as a general guide each mah of battery rating equals 1 pellet that the gun will fire. So a battery with a rating of 2000 mah = 2000 pellets you can fire before battery life runs out.

Note: A semi-automatic gun means that pulling the trigger will fire a single shot or sometimes a burst of 2-3 rounds where as a fully automatic gun would fire a continuous burst of rounds with a single pull and hold of the trigger and only stop firing when the trigger is released.

TOP TIP: Note that in cold weather conditions and electric operating system would be a better option than gas powered as the cold conditions will not affect the operation like gas operated systems will.

Silencer

Just a quick note on airsoft silencers. A silencer is a tubular barrel extension that is meant to suppress the noise that the rifle makes when firing so as not to give away your position or make people aware of your presence.
However, although a silencer on an airsoft gun may look great, they don't generally do much to suppress the noise, although it may actually increase the accuracy and range of the gun slightly.

TOP TIP: To aid in noise suppression, some foam wrapped around the gearbox can dramatically reduce the noise of the weapon firing.

Sling

It's important that you have a good sling on your sniper rifle. This will provide you with a way of carrying the rifle when it's not required and therefore leaves both of your hands free to do other things like use binoculars, use a map and compass etc

TOP TIP: As well as this, the sling can also be used to aid you in providing stability and improving accuracy of different firing positions.

Ammunition

It's very important to choose the right ammunition for your rifle as it will make all the difference to the range and accuracy of your shots. Airsoft ammo range from the lightweight, low quality and less expensive to the higher quality and heavier type.

The weights of BB pellets range from .12 grams which are cheaper but provide poor accuracy to the heavier .30 grams which a far more accurate but they may slightly reduce the range.
There are weights in between but I'd recommend using .25 grams for the sniper rifle. When checking the ammo avoid any BB pellets which seem poorly made with visible seams, cracks or any other imperfections.

Using high quality ammo and a good sniper rifle you could expect to hit a target up to around 91metres (300 feet) away or with an extremely upgraded rifle up to 121m (400 feet) this would have to be perfect firing conditions though.

Camouflage

As well as wearing camouflage clothing it is vital to also camouflage is your rifle to prevent giving away your position.

This should be done sticking coloured tape over any shiny surfaces as well as to the stock and barrel; this will help break up any solid colours.
You should also wrap materials such as scrim/vehicle netting around various parts of the rifle but make sure that none of these prevent the working parts from operating properly or prevent you from assembling/disassembling your rifle for cleaning etc.
If there are any parts of your rifle that are likely to heat up after excessive firing, then avoid putting any flammable materials on them.

Rifle Scope & Aiming

The sniper rifle scope is a vital piece of equipment as without this it's unlikely you'll hit any targets at long range. It's essential that the sight and rifle are zeroed correctly.

This means that prior to playing or using your rifle, you have used your rifle on a target range and made the necessary adjustments to your sight, so that where you are aiming when looking through the scope is exactly where you're round lands.
You may still be hitting the target but if your scope is only very slightly off centre at a short distance, this would mean that at greater distance it is far more off centre and you would miss the target completely.

How to Zero Your Scope

To zero your scope you will need to place a target at a set distance, let's say 100 metres.

Now from a set firing position, preferably the prone (lying on your stomach) position.

Aim at the centre of the target and fire 5-10 shots

If you're totally missing the target look at where your rounds are landing and adjust the scope as necessary. So if the rounds are landing a metre to the left adjust the sight to bring it over to the right by 1m.

Once you are hitting the target if the rounds are hitting it all over the place, ensure all fittings are tight and if they are, then you may need t work on your shooting skills!?
(I'll help you with this later)

Now, once you are hitting the target and managing to get all of your rounds in roughly the same area (this is called a grouping) try to get your grouping as tight as possible.
(Just to give you an idea of what I mean, I used to get 10 rounds in a grouping the size of a large coin from 600 metres, this was obviously a military sniper rifle I was using firing live rounds).

So now you have a good grouping, you need to see where the centre of that group lies (this is the mean point of impact) and then make the necessary adjustments to your scope, to move that mean point of impact over to the centre of the target.

You may need to do this a few times until the majority of your rounds are landing exactly where you are aiming and hitting the dead centre of the target.

Aiming

Unlike fixed iron sights on a gun where there is a sight on the front and rear, and should be aimed so that the front sight is between the gap of the rear sight and level with it also.
The telescopic scope provides a far more accurate aim especially at targets that are some distance away. Some targets probably wouldn't even be seen at very long distances by the naked eye.
There are many different types of rifle scopes all with different reticles.

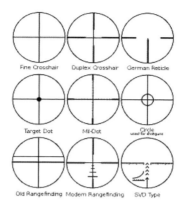

Fine Crosshair   Duplex Crosshair   German Reticle

Target Dot   Mil-Dot   Circle used for shotguns

Old Rangefinding   Modern Rangefinding   SVD Type

Above: Here you can see a number of different reticles that you would see through the sights of various rifle scopes.

Some reticles have various lines or arrows to assist the sniper in measuring the distance away from the target. These may be used as well as the assistance of a spotter if the sniper is operating in a 2 man team.

The scope view below shows the reticle of a Schmidt & Bender 3-12x 50 telescopic sights. As you can see there are Mil-dots on the cross hairs and lines underneath. On the diagram below it: You can see how the head of a helmeted man fits between the horizontal and ascending lines, thus indicating how many metres away he is. (Note for a head they start at 100m and increase by 50m up to 250m)
If you are judging the distance of a a person standing then the upper body only should be placed within these lines and the distance starts at 400m increasing by 200m intervals up to 100m away.

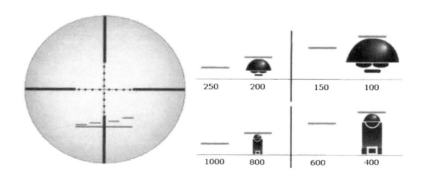

250   200   150   100

1000   800   600   400

Below is an image taken through a sniper scope, as you can see from the hills in the background the target is some distance away, maybe around 300m and another approx 450m away with dead ground in between them.

Night Vision

There is a vast selection of night vision devices (NVD's) available to both the military and the public. These devices can be narrowed down to just 3 main categories, these being; Cameras, Binoculars and Scopes.
The only one that we will be concerned with for the purpose of sniping will be the Scope.

Now, if money is no object to you then you might consider purchasing a form of night vision scope. This would obviously put you at a distinct advantage over your opponents who are unlikely to have NVD's but they can be quite expensive.
Some scopes provide not only the ability to see in the dark but also incorporate sighting reticles so you can aim at targets in the dark too.
As with your sniper scope, this NVD will need to be zeroed correctly in the same way but at night.

As you can imagine, this is quite a powerful position to be in. Not only are you totally hidden from your opponents but you can witness them fumbling around in the dark whilst you take your time observing them before deciding which one of them you are going to eliminate, you take your shot and they're gone!

Whilst the rest of their team run for cover wondering what the hell just happened and where did the shot come from.

Above: The view you can see is of a line of troops on the move at night, you can see each individual soldier. Without the aid of night vision its unlikely you would see these at all.

NVD's can work in 2 ways:

Thermal Imaging

A thermal imaging device picks up on heat that is emitted from an object or person. It can be set to show heat in reds with other cooler areas in greens and blues. Or it can be set to black and white which shows heat as white. The stronger or brighter the white (or red in infrared) then the hotter the image is.

Image Enhancement An Image Enhancement Device works by collecting tiny amounts of light that is invisible to the human eye and amplifying it so as we can identify the object.

Side Arm

Generally speaking a sniper doesn't usually carry a side arm such as a pistol. It's very rare that they will be operating anywhere near the distance that a pistol can fire and if they are that close, it's probably because things haven't gone quite according to plan.

However, in some instances it may come in handy to have a side arm especially in the confines of playing an airsoft game. You may be confronted by an opponent at short range and a pistol can be used quicker and easier to lay down a few rounds to aid your escape or even take out an opponent if you are skilled and can accurately use one.

As pistols are smaller than rifles and an electric pistol would have a smaller battery, then the firepower would only provide 200-280 fps and be used at close range.

A pistol magazine can be a single stack mag holding from 7-20 rounds (BB's) or a double stack magazine can hold up to 30 rounds of ammunition.

When firing a pistol hold the firing arm out straight but very slightly bent, aiming towards the target with the hand grasping the handle and finger on the trigger.
Your other hand should grasp the bottom of the pistol grip underneath your firing hand so as to steady the weapon and assist in the stability of your aim.
When squeezing the trigger, avoid squeezing it quickly. Aim using the iron sights on the top of the pitol and slowly squeeze the trigger, this will help maintain your aim and make sure you hit the target in the area you are aiming at.

Radio Communications

It's essential that you have some form of radio communication with the rest of your team. You will also need an ear piece and possible a throat mic.
It's likely that you be operating separately and some distance away so you will need to keep in contact with them, you may need to relay information back to them or find out their location or time of attack.
It's no good having a radio without an earpiece as you would otherwise have to turn up the volume high enough for you to hear and this could mean others could hear it too.
It's more convenient to have a throat mic too and it also allows you to speak quietly on the radio and still be heard.

Camouflage Cream

Even though you have your ghillie suit, gloves and boots all camouflaged it's also important to wear a good camouflage cream that won't come off easily whilst sweating.
I know that you will also be wearing goggles or a facemask but your skin needs to be camouflaged too.

I've seen alot of pictures on the internet of people wearing very impressive ghillie suits that are probably very effective, only to spoil it by not having their face camouflaged.
Your skin does not blend with your surroundings and can actually give away your position quite easily. The skin reflects light slightly and more so when you've been sweating. The areas to pay attention to are the forehead, cheek bones, jaw and chin. Not forgetting your ears and neck.

The best way to apply it is to cover your entire face, ears and neck with a very thin layer of cammo cream (I know it doesn't sound pleasant but we used to rub cammo cream into our hands then use spit to water it down a bit before applying it)
Then use the stick or your fingers to apply the cream to the specific areas of your face using any design you like and there are many styles to choose from.

Above: Here you can see just 2 different styles of applying your Cam Cream, the options are endless.

Watch

You should ensure that you wear a water resistant watch and possibly shock proof too as it's going to get bumped and scraped. This will be necessary not only to tell the time but it's also likely that you will have been given various timings by your team commander for things like when you should reach your target and be in position or what time the team are going to be assaulting the enemy position or carrying out an ambush.
During the team briefing it's likely that all players will synchronise their watches so that they are all exactly the same.

Compass

Having a compass is essential for you to navigate and will be used in conjunction with a map to plan your route and locate your opponents known position.
You may be given a grid reference of where you are required to set up an observation post or observe an area that the enemy are likely to use.
Without a compass this would be near impossible and you could end up totally disoriented and lost.

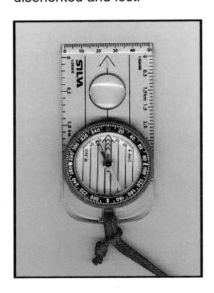

Protractor

A protractor is used with a map and compass to determine the angular direction between two given points on a map. This will allow you to adjust your compass and aid in your navigation.
It may also be used to determine your arcs of fire and field of view from your position. If you were to relay a message to your team commander you could give them your exact location and give them your field of view using the angles on the protractor so that they could then mark it on the map and have a visual aid as to what area you can cover.
I would advise that you use a circular protractor rather than a semi-circular one. It provides you with 360 degrees and will help with more accurate readings.

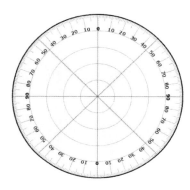

Pen and Notebook

You will need some way of making notes and recording information so that you don't forget it.

You will also need to produce panoramic sketches of what you can see from your fire position. Don't worry; you do not need to be an artist. Just a rough drawing of what you can see in as much perspective as possible will do. So objects further away will appear smaller etc. This will aid you in providing information to your team as well as making a note of the distances to key reference points. For example, judging the distance to a building in the distance and making a note of it on the drawing, will assist you in engaging a target quicker if one appears near that location.

Water

It's vital that you carry some form of water carrier so that you can drink when you need to. You may be deployed for some time and with all the walking and crawling you'll be doing, it's likely you'll be sweating. You do not want to become dehydrated as this may cause you to become irritable, get a headache etc and would therefore effect your performance.

The Skills of a Sniper

To become a fully competent and effective sniper, there are 7 essential skills that you should master. Each one of these plays a very important part in your overall performance.

These skills are;

Shooting
Camouflage & Concealment
Observation
Judging Distance
Map Reading
Stalking
Sniper Knowledge (Although an excellent level of sniper knowledge is required covering all areas of equipment statistics and mechanisms as well as use of air photographs etc are required for a military sniper, for the purpose of this book on airsoft sniping I will avoid filling your head with information that you don't really need)

All of these skills will be covered in this book.

Following an official military sniper training course, there are 3 ways in which you can be graded and these are;

    FAIL
    PASS
    PASS SNIPER MARKSMAN

Failing any one of the above skills results in overall failure of the whole course and if you are aiming to receive your 'Sniper Marksman Badge' then you are required to achieve top marks and the grade of pass sniper marksman in every one of the skills.

This is far from easy and as you can imagine after all their hard work, there are a few unhappy faces after people have been told that they were very good at everything apart from, for example Judging distance and therefore failed.

Obviously as an airsoft sniper there may be one or two of these skills that aren't as important to you, however if you want to be feared on the battlefield and be the best sniper that you can be, then mastering the majority of them will help you no end.

With that said, let's get started!

Shooting

As you are reading this book I am assuming that you are already a relatively good shot. However, if you are not then this section will help you become one.
For those of you that are this section is aimed to helping you improve your shooting skills and you may learn a few things that you may not already be aware of.

There are 3 main basic essentials required for good shooting;

    You will need to be in a comfortable firing position.

    You need to ensure that you have a very stable firing position to avoid un-necessary movement.

    You need the correct sight alignment to ensure the correct aim and fire the weapon without disturbing your aim.

So, whenever you are getting in position to take a shot think about how long you may be in this position for and to avoid any possible movement that could affect your shot try to remember this checklist.

Fire Position Checklist:

When in a firing position you should ensure that you are in a comfortable position and it's unlikely to become uncomfortable by causing any aches or pains in your joints.

Think about stability for example if you are lying down have you elbows firmly planted on the ground or surface where it is unlikely that they will slip and not too close together or far apart.

Your front arm should be extended so that your front hand is holding the rifle as far enough away as necessary to prevent the end of the rifle from dropping slightly

You should have a firm grip with the other hand around the firing handle and pull it back slightly so that the rifle butt is firmly tucked in against you shoulder

Your eye should be far enough away from the scope so that the scope doesn't hit your eye due to the recoil after taking a shot

Make sure that you have a clear view straight through the scope and that there are no thick black shadows around the inside of the scope. This would indicate that your eye is not aligned correctly and you will need to adjust your position slightly until it's gone.

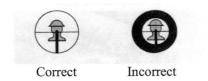

Correct   Incorrect

Correctly breathing whilst aiming is very important. Take slow breaths and then when exhaling stop just short of breathing out and hold your breath just prior to taking the shot. Do Not hold your breath too long however as this will result in strain and will affect your shot. Just exhale normally and start again

The trigger operation is one of the most important elements to good marksmanship. You should use the first joint of your finger and not the tip and apply pressure to the bottom of the trigger.
Then slowly and very gradually squeeze the trigger until you take up the initial pressure until you feel the second pressure then continue slowly squeezing until the shot is fired

If you are aiming at a moving target, aim slightly in front of the target depending on which way it's travelling and at what speed. For a person walking at 200m away then aim about half the targets width in front of them, if they're running then aim about the full targets width in front of them

Things to avoid

Avoid snatching the trigger or squeezing it too quickly as this will disturb your aim

Avoid flinching whilst taking the shot, you know it's going to go BANG so just relax

Don't hesitate or dwell too long on a shot, the longer you take the more likely your aim will be effected

Make sure you have a firm grip with your firing hand prior to squeezing the rigger so that you can feel the trigger pressure correctly

Make sure that your rifle and scope are cleaned and working properly and that all securing screws are tightened prior to use

Safety Regulations

Whilst not actively playing ensure that you cover the end of your rifle with a bag or sock and secure it with an elastic band

Whilst not in play remove the magazine and fire of the action straight up into the air.

When not shooting make sure your rifle's safety catch is set to the safe position Never intentionally fire the rifle at very close range especially at an opponents face

Only use the correct form of ammunition designed for the rifle

Shooting Conditions

There are many factors that may influence your shot. If you follow the fire position checklist provided and there are no adverse conditions then your shots should be very similar. However you may need to take into account other factors that can effect shooting but be careful not to over compensate for these, as this is quite a common mistake. Here's a list of common conditions that may affect your shooting;

Wind

This can be a common problem especially effecting low quality BB's and can lead to missing the target completely. Wind can not only affect the flight and speed of the BB but also the snipers firing position too.
Try looking out for signs that tell the wind direction and strength such as trees, plants or even things like flags blowing in the wind. You could use methods like throwing grass up in the air to see which way it blows but remember the wind conditions where your target is may differ from your location. So look for signs near your target and make the necessary adjustments.

Temperature

You should avoid leaving your rifle or ammunition in a position that is exposed to heat from the sun for too long. It will have an effect on that side of the rifle's barrel and affect the shot. Hot conditions will increase the rifles muzzle velocity which will mean you will need to aim slightly lower or adjust your scope and therefore in cold conditions you will need to increase your elevation

Mirage

On a very hot day you may have noticed that sometimes there are visible waves low down to the ground. This is caused by the hot temperatures and in little or no wind conditions the waves appear to raise vertically or when there is a wind the waves drift in that direction. Adjustments should therefore be made as necessary.

Humidity

For long range shooting you should be aware that a high level of humidity in the air will cause more downward pressure on your BB's so in this case you should aim slightly higher or adjust your scopes elevation

Rain

You should always carry a clean cloth to dry your weapon, scope lens and ammunition. It's a good idea to make a make-shift cover over the end of your scope's lens as this will help prevent the rain hitting it as well as sunlight reflecting of it. This can easily be done by using cardboard or plastic and securing it with some elastic bands

Light

Light can influence people in different ways so it's best to make note of how you shoot in dull poor lit conditions as well as bright conditions. People tend to aim higher in poorly lit conditions and higher in bright ones but you will only know how it affects you with practice

Clothing

Regardless of the weather conditions it's always advisable to wear the correct form of clothing that a sniper requires. Don't decide that because it's too hot, you'll dress down as this will not only effect you camouflage but also it leaves you open to sun burn, insect bites, stings etc

Fire Positions

There are a number of different firing positions you can use but with each one try to remember the fire position checklist I gave you earlier. This will help make sure your position allows you to take an accurate shot as possible. Incorporated with each of these positions I advise that you use the sling to improve stability. If you have a bipod attached to your rifle this can help a lot or you can use any available cover or platform to assist you.

The firing positions I will cover are;

    Standing
    Kneeling
    Sitting
    Lying Back
    Lying/Prone Position
    The Hawkins Position

Standing

One of the most difficult positions to use whilst maintaining a good accurate aim is the standing position. There are times when you may not have any other options so plenty of practice is required. If there is any cover such as a tree that you can lean against then this may help. Avoid resting your rifle on top of any cover where you can easily be seen by the enemy, this is where your background may help camouflage you.

In an un-supported firing position, stand side on, shoulder width apart and aim at your target. The main point to remember with this position is to make sure that your supporting arm has your elbow tucked in tight to your body which means that your supporting hand will be closer to the firing hand. You could also use your upper arm behind the elbow to pull the sling taught which can help with stability.

Kneeling

The kneeling position should never be used on sloping ground and is slightly easier than standing but is still quite difficult to maintain a good level of stability.

You may also find that it causes your rear foot to ache and can be uncomfortable after a while. There are 3 ways in which you can position your rear foot;

> Sitting back on your heel with the toes on the ground pointing straight back
> Sitting back on your heel using the ball of your foot on the ground
> Turning your foot inwards so that you sit back on the inside of your foot

> Hold the rifle in the with your supporting arm extended and your hand on the stock further away and place your elbow behind your knee

TOP TIP: Never place the bone of your elbow on the bone of your knee cap as it's likely to move and ruin your shot.

Sitting

The sitting position is more comfortable but you should avoid using it on sloping ground.
Sit on the ground with both legs out in front of you just over shoulder width apart and ensure your heels are dug into the ground. Then aim as you did before placing both elbows behind each knee. You can adjust this position by crossing your feet or even sitting cross legged, just choose which ever is more comfortable for you.

Lying Back

Lying back is a very comfortable position although after a while you may feel a strain in your neck and shoulders. You should lie back on side with your leading leg bent slightly and at a 45 degree angle to the ground. Use the outside of your upper most knee to rest your rifle on and ensure that the sling goes around the front of that knee. If you're right handed then you'll be leaning back on your right and supporting yourself on your right elbow, with your left hand on the top of the rifle but securing it into your right shoulder.

Lying/Prone Position

This is probably the most common and accurate firing position as well being the best position to limit the chance of you being seen.
Lie on the ground face down and aim the rifle as you would normally. Place your supporting hand down towards the end of the stock and make sure both elbows are just over shoulder width apart, in a stable position and unlikely to move or slip. The upper arm can again be used to pull the sling taught and make sure that the rifle butt is tight in against your shoulder and your cheek is resting on the butt far enough away to leave you with the correct eye relief from the scope.
You can have both legs straight out behind you or...

TOP TIP: Bring your right knee up to the side so that it points out to your right. This should bring your belly off the ground slightly and prevent any movement as you breathe to affect your shot.

The Hawkins Position

This is very similar to the prone position however the advantage of this position is that you are lower down to the ground which helps conceal you more than the normal prone position. The placement of your supporting hand also provides a much more stable platform and can improve accuracy.
The only difference is that you position your body so that you are laying side on to the target, as opposed to your legs being straight out behind you and with your supporting arm is laying flat on the ground with your leading hand side on and clenching the front sling attachment to form a stable platform.

Camouflage & Concealment

One of the most impressive and exceptional skills that a sniper possess, is the ability to remain hidden and undetected from his enemy whilst he moves silently through his environment and locates, observes and eliminates his target. Leaving no trace that he was ever there. It causes fear in the enemy knowing that, at any moment they could be shot by a single round from a great distance and not have any idea of what just happened or where the shot came from.

The best examples of camouflage can be seen by observing wildlife and animals that depend on their camouflage for their own survival. Much like a chameleon adapts it's own natural camouflage to that of it's surroundings, you too will need to do the same to ensure you remain hidden.
This can be done by using camouflage cream to cover areas of your skin as well as wearing camouflage clothing such as a ghillie suit. (For more details on camouflaging yourself and your equipment please refer back to the sniper equipment section).
However, there's far more to camouflage and concealment than just what you wear and how you look.

Use of Cover

No matter how well you manage to camouflage yourself, your efforts will be wasted unless you know how to use all available elements of cover correctly. With experience, this skill will become second nature and you will be able to identify the best route to take and most suitable location to hide yourself far quicker and easier. The following list will provide you with the necessary elements of cover that you will need to consider when moving or taking up a firing/observation position.

Dead Ground

When planning a route or moving from one position to another always try an use the grounds natural contours to aid you in staying out of sight of the enemy. This could be done by moving around an area of raised ground instead of walking over it or using valleys or dips in the ground to get to where you are going. This is also a lot faster than having to crawl to get there. When planning your route using a map make a note of the contour lines and plan your route accordingly.

Movement

Always assume that whenever you move that the area is under observation from your opponents. Before you decide to move, always have a planned route no matter how short the distance and a point in which you are aiming for. Make a note of any available areas of cover that you intend to use. Once you reach your destination then do the same for your next movement. The areas of cover you have already made a mental note of will come in handy if you need to hide quickly.

Noise

Use any noise such as overhead aircraft, gunfire or anything else that may distract your enemy to help conceal the noise of your movement. When walking through areas such as woods where you could step on some wood and snap it or other surfaces that could alert someone, first use the front outer edge of your leading foot to sweep the area before putting your weight on to it. Be aware that making a noise such as a snapping twig may not be heard by your opponents but when it causes birds or other wildlife to scatter it will be noticed!

Isolated Cover

Avoid isolated cover where there are limited areas of cover available. This means that if you are moving across a field for example and there is one tree in the centre, don't use this as cover as it is very obvious and your opponents will pick up on this and watch it carefully.

Soft Cover

Whenever there is soft cover available such as shrubs or old wooden fences, you should try to observe or shoot through it instead of looking over the top of it.

Background

As well as trying to blend in with the cover in front of you, it's also important to consider your background. If you are blending in with the lighter ground in front of you but your background is darker then it may be possible for the enemy to make out your shape or pick up on something that just doesn't look right.

Silhouette

It's very easy to see a person's silhouette as they move along the crest of a hill or any high ground even from a long distance and especially at night. So avoid moving over the top of hills and walk along the side of a hill further down.

Shadow

Using shadows is a great way of using naturally created cover although you need to stay aware of the sun's movement and how the shadow moves also otherwise you will alter the natural shape of the shadow.

Foliage

The use of natural foliage for camouflage is essential to maintaining your concealment as you move through different environments. As your surroundings change, you should remove the foliage you were using and replace it with that of your new surroundings. Also be aware that in time foliage will dry and die which means it may change colour and not blend in, so you may need to replace it.

Movement

There are a few different methods of movement you can use depending on your given location and any available cover that you find.
Obviously, the closer you get to your opponents the more stealthily you will need to become.
The methods you can use are described below:

The Monkey Run

This is probably the first method you will use as you attempt to get closer to your fire/observation position without being seen. It's done by crawling on your knees using your right hand/fist to support you and holding your rifle in your left hand making sure you keep it low down and parallel.

The leopard Crawl

This is done by lying flat on the ground and supporting your upper body on your elbows, grasping the front sling attachment of your rifle with your right hand and the rifle lying on the ground beside you. You then bring up your right knee to your side and push off it moving your body and your right elbow forward until your right leg is straight and you come to rest on your right elbow and the right side of your body. You then repeat the exact same process with your left side and so on...

The Stomach Crawl

This method will provide you with the best possible cover and minimal chance of making any noise but it is very slow. As a military sniper you are sometimes left with no other option but to use this method to travel some considerable distances, as not doing so could result in you being shot and then it's literally game over!

The way to do this is to lay flat on your stomach with your head low to the ground and your arms outstretched in front of you. You then use your fingers to try and gain a grip of the ground and pull yourself forward keeping your elbows out to the side so that you don't raise your body off the ground and the rest of your body drags flat along the ground. Using this method whilst carrying a rifle is done in just the same way but you hold your rifle on the ground in front of the centre of your body pointing out in front of you. As you move forward your chest comes to rest on the rifle butt then you move it forward again.

Here you can see a demonstration of the stomach crawl whilst carrying a rifle.

Observation

Observation is a key skill for the sniper and there are many different ways in which it can help you achieve your goal. Without excellent observation skills you are unlikely to reach your destination without putting yourself in a position that might be being observed by your opponents. If you can see your opponents before they see you, then you have a distinct advantage over them.

Your task may even be to go out and gather intelligence and information without being given a target to engage. This information may play a vital role in your teams attack plans and overall success. Imagine the satisfaction of knowing that with your help and input your whole team could win the game and minimise the chances of your team members being shot. You would be one very popular and respected player!

Through the use of observation equipment such as binoculars and sniper scopes you can locate the enemy early on whilst they are completely unaware of you watching them and use your skills to advise your team commander of possible attack options or locate designated targets that when eliminated will give your team an advantage over them.

As part of your observation skills you may also need to sketch a rough panoramic picture of what you can see (I mentioned this briefly earlier).
Just to give you an idea of what I mean, I've drawn a very rough example which took only a few seconds to do and I made up an image of the top of my head. So you'll have to excuse how basic it is but it is just to show that you don't actually need to be any good at drawing.

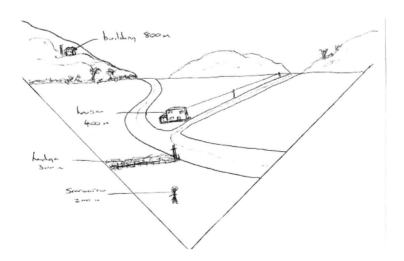

Note that I've recorded the known distances to various easily identifiable reference points. This will aid you with any target identification.

Target Identification

With target identification there are set methods to use so that everyone is working off the same method and understands any identification instructions given. You may well be working in a sniper team which means you will be in a pair and have a spotter to assist you. So you will need to be easily able to quickly identify a target that he sees where ever they are and what ever distance away they might be.

The 3 main methods of indication given are;

Range

A spotter may give you an estimated range as accurately as possible to a target or reference point. This is mainly to get you looking at the right distance away and it's then up to you to judge the distance and make any adjustments necessary. You are the one taking the shot so it's your responsibility to get it right.

Wind

The spotter will give you an indication of the wind speed and direction. You will also need to judge this for yourself and use any available signs to gauge it as accurately as possible. With both yours and the spotters assessment you should have quite an accurate reading in which to make your adjustments.

Indication

Using the rough sketch I did, the target indication given between a spotter and sniper would go something like this;

Spotter: "400 metres, House, Right 2 o'clock, 1st telegraph pole, bottom right, Enemy"

Sniper: " I see him, are you ready?"

Spotter: "Ok...Fire when ready".

The reason that the sniper asks if the spotter is ready, is so that if he misses the target then the spotter can see where the round landed and inform the sniper of the necessary adjustments he needs to make.

When the spotter says 2'oclock for example what he is using is the clock method. What this means is that when he identifies a specific reference point such as the house, you should picture that object to be in the centre of an imaginary clock face. Then judge where the number 2 would be and follow an imaginary line from the object in the centre along that line until you see the 1st telegraph pole.

Judging Distance

Being able to accurately judge distances in various conditions is a vital skill that the sniper must master. If you are lucky enough to possess a laser range finder or binoculars with a range finder in built then that's great and will assist you no end and make life a lot easier but if you rely on it and it becomes damaged or fails to work properly then you're in trouble. This is why you still need to make sure that you are able to use the various methods of judging using only the naked eye, binoculars and scope.
The following methods can be used;

Unit of Measure

This is where you take a known distance of an area such as a football/soccer pitch which equals 100 metres. Then imagine how many times it would fit in between you and the target. Breaking it down into halves (50m) or Quarters (25m) if necessary the closer you get to the target.

Appearance Method

Using this method requires you to know the size of certain object such as a person or an average size house at specific distances.
So for example you remember a visual image of how big a person looks whilst standing at 200 metres away and the difference in size if they are 300 metres away etc.

Halving Method

This is where you already know an accurate distance to a specific reference point and you then half that distance so it's roughly in line with the target.

Bracketing Method

This is where you judge the target to be no more than X metres and no less than Y metres and use the measurement in between.

Squad Average

If you are operating within a team then you can use the squad average method. This means each member estimates the distance to a target and you use the average measurement.

Binocular/Scope Graticules

As explained in the sniper equipment section covering these pieces of equipment, the graticules can be used to judge the distance to a target.

Map Reading

The ability to quickly and accurately read a map is a very important skill that a sniper must master and can often overlooked. You could be the best shot in the world but if you can't make your way to where you need to be without getting lost or taking the wrong route then you're not going to be much use.

You should take every opportunity to practice your map reading skills outdoors using both a compass and protractor until you feel completely confident in your ability and never left unsure that you're making the right decision whilst planning your route.

There are several examples of how good map reading will benefit you as a sniper, these are;

Selecting the best possible route to a given location, fire position or observation post.
Determining how long it's likely to take you to get to a location over various terrains
Choosing a good site for an observation post or firing position
Judging the distance from an observation/firing position to a target
Providing information and recording an accurate log or report

Using a map effectively requires the sniper be competent in understanding;

The Grid System and Bearings

When given co-ordinates of a target or location you should be able to use the grid system and bearings to accurately identify the correct location.

Symbols and Scales

You should know how all of the symbols on a map are used to identify various landmarks. You should also be able to use the scales to judge distances and the approximate time it would take at different speeds to get from one to another.

Stalking

This is it, now is the time when every aspect of your training comes in to play!

When you first begin playing an airsoft game then it may be likely that you are some distance away from your opponents. However, as you get closer you will need to adapt your movements accordingly. So, you might start off by running to get within a certain distance of your enemy as quick as possible and they may be doing the same.
As you're approaching the mid way point you may choose to slow down to a brisk walk whilst map reading and planning your route using your binoculars and scope to scan the ground in the distance for any available cover and signs of the enemy.

As you get closer still, you will need to consider crawling and start using any available cover you find. During the later stages it's likely that you may have noticed or located your opponent's position and you will now need to use all of your camouflage and concealment skills to ensure that you remain un-detected. Bear in mind that your opponents will also be using visual aids such as binoculars and scopes to try and locate you (Maybe even night vision devices but hopefully not).

So now you're within distance of taking a shot. You will be slowly and silently moving along the ground, praying that nothing gives away your location after all the hard work you have put in to get so close to your target without being noticed.

As you find the perfect location to take up a firing position you feel confident that due to your amazing ability to blend in so perfectly with your surroundings, it feels almost as if you are invisible.

You use your expert judgement of distances to accurately gauge the range between you and your target.

Now you have your target in your sights, you can feel the adrenaline pumping through your veins. You are waiting for that perfect opportunity to engage the target. Will it be a head shot or chest? You steady your breathing and take up the pressure of the trigger.

It all boils down to this one shot as you slowly squeeze the trigger.....

TARGET DOWN!!

You did it!

One shot - One Kill

You see the impact of your round hit the enemy target and you have a confirmed kill!

Are you going to get the hell out of there or do you decide to stick around a bit longer and see how many more targets you can take out?

About the Author

On the 20th April 1991 at the age of 17, I applied to join the Coldstream Guards. An Elite Infantry Regiment that not only fights overseas but whilst based in London, England, their Primary role is to carry out Ceremonial Duties and Guard the Royal Family and their properties.
I served operationally on several tours of duty and worked in various hostile environments as well as working in jungle and arctic conditions.

Joining the Armed Forces was all I had ever dreamt of doing and if I was to do this, I didn't want to just join any regiment. I intended to join one of the most elite and respected Regiments in the British Army. This meant that I spent a lot of time as a teenager improving my fitness, as well as reading all about military skills that I knew one day would help me achieve my goal.

Right from an early age my childhood was very hard and unsettled in many ways. Maybe my decision to join the armed forces was in my blood or just a way of escaping?
I had never known my Father, who had also served in the Coldstream Guards but I had a very loving and caring Aunt and Uncle that took care of me when my mother couldn't due to her illness. My Uncle became the closest thing I ever had to a Father and he used to help me prepare for the gruelling training that I would face.
He'd drive me out 7-8 miles into the countryside in the winter, drop me off in the middle of nowhere then drive home and time how long it took me to run back.
(At least that's what he told me ;)
I remember on one occasion we found a long stretch of straight road that stretched about 3 miles, I decided it would be a challenge to see if I could push the car that far, which I managed to do but we kept having people stop to ask us if we needed a hand, they must've thought we were mad!?

Even before I had started my initial basic infantry training, I already had specific ambitions that I wanted to achieve within the Military.
I wanted to travel and see the world, serve my country but my main ambition was to become a Sniper.
To me, a Sniper was like the ultimate soldier, able to work alone and remain undetected whilst eliminating enemy targets or gathering important military information, then returning to their unit after successfully completing their mission.

The guards is one of the most disciplined regiments in the world and at the time I was totally unaware that all of this discipline and being made to stand motionless for hours on parade, would actually help me develop the self discipline and patience it takes to become a good sniper.

Whenever we were on the ranges I would notice Snipers in their ghillie suits practicing their shooting and feel a kind of jealousy that it wasn't me. I admired how professional they appeared and imagined what it's like to be one of them. Watching them, easily dropping targets that I could barely see in the distance.

It wasn't long before my shooting ability was noticed on the ranges and after coming 2nd out of almost 1000 members of various regiments in an all services shooting competition I was soon selected to attend a sniper training course.

After passing the course and receiving the much sought after Sniper Marksman Badge,
I was attached to the reconnaissance platoon where I operated as a sniper and carried out further operational tours of duty and other forms of training in various areas.

I had finally achieved my goal which I'd dreamt about for so many years.

I was a Sniper!

Dedication

I would like to dedicate this book to my
Aunt and Uncle

Mr. and Mrs. Rock

Who cared for and supported me during the many years of my childhood
from an early age.
Without whom I wouldn't be the person
I am today.
They are like the only parents I have and I love them both dearly
Their dedication to helping others
I try to follow.

Copyright, Legal Notice and Disclaimer

Printed in Great Britain
by Amazon.co.uk, Ltd.,
Marston Gate.